TURNING POINTS

THE ASSASSINATION OF JOHN F. KENNEDY

BY VALERIE BODDEN

CREATIVE EDUCATION • CREATIVE PAPERBACKS

Published by Creative Education and Creative Paperbacks
P.O. Box 227, Mankato, Minnesota 56002
Creative Education and Creative Paperbacks are imprints of
The Creative Company
www.thecreativecompany.us

Design and production by The Design Lab
Art direction by Rita Marshall
Printed in China

Photographs by Corbis (Bettmann, Corbis, dpa/dpa, Schulman-Sachs/
dpa, Ted Spiegel), Creative Commons Wikimedia (Heinz Junge/Deutsches
Bundesarchiv, Arnold Newman/WHPO, Cecil Stoughton/White House, Texas
State Archives, U.S. Army Signal Corps), Design Lab, Dreamstime (Lori Ferber),
John F. Kennedy Presidential Library & Museum (Abbie Rowe/White House
Photographs, Cecil W. Stoughton/White House Photographs), Library of
Congress (Orlando Fernandez/NYWTS/PPOC, NYWTS/PPOC), Shutterstock
(Eldad Carin, Joseph Sohm)

Library of Congress Cataloging-in-Publication Data
Bodden, Valerie.
The assassination of John F. Kennedy / Valerie Bodden.
p. cm. — (Turning points)
Includes bibliographical references and index.
Summary: A historical account of John F. Kennedy's assassination, including the
events leading up to it, the people involved, conspiracy theories surrounding his
death, and the lingering aftermath.

ISBN 978-1-60818-746-1 (hardcover)
ISBN 978-1-62832-342-9 (pbk)
ISBN 978-1-56660-781-0 (eBook)
Kennedy, John F. (John Fitzgerald), 1917–1963—Assassination—Juvenile
literature.

E842.Z9 B63 2016
973.922092—dc23   2016000354

CCSS: RI.5.1, 2, 3, 8; RI. 6.1, 2, 4, 7; RH.6-8.3, 4, 5, 6, 7, 8

First Edition HC 9 8 7 6 5 4 3 2 1
First Edition PBK 9 8 7 6 5 4 3 2 1

Cover, main image, and this page: John F. Kennedy at a presidential
campaign stop in Seattle, Washington

TABLE *of* CONTENTS

When president John F. Kennedy set out for a campaign stop in Texas in November 1963, he was at the height of his popularity. He had been in office just over 1,000 days, but the American people loved him. The president was young and energetic, and he had promised to "get the country moving again." Texans were well known for their resistance to the president, but the trip started out well. Then, in Dallas on November 22, things went horribly wrong. As the president and his wife, Jacqueline, traveled through the city's streets in their open-topped limousine, an assassin took three shots at their car. Two hit the president, killing him.

Within minutes, television and radio stations delivered the news across the country. People everywhere were stunned. Most would never forget where they were when they heard the news. Millions watched the president's funeral on television.

And millions were also tuned in when Lee Harvey Oswald, the man who had been arrested for the assassination, was murdered on live TV. Oswald's death left many suspicious that Kennedy's assassination had been a **conspiracy**. The debate about this turning point in American history rages on more than 50 years later.

President Kennedy and his wife descended the steps of Air Force One in good spirits shortly before noon.

As a result of his debates with Kennedy, Nixon did not participate in televised debates during later campaigns.

CHAPTER ONE

A NEW ERA

John F. Kennedy's road to the presidency began in 1944. That year, his older brother, Joseph Jr., was killed in World War II. Joseph had always planned to enter politics, and John Kennedy picked up where his brother had left off. Soon after fighting in the war himself, Kennedy began a 14-year career in Congress. He served first in the House and then in the Senate. In 1960, he entered the presidential race as a candidate for the Democratic Party. He clinched the party's nomination at the Democratic National Convention and asked fellow candidate Lyndon B. Johnson to be his running mate.

On September 26, 1960, more than 70 million people across the country watched as Kennedy and his opponent, Republican Richard Nixon, took part in the first-ever televised presidential debate. On TV, Kennedy came across as relaxed, athletic, and charming. Nixon, on the other hand, seemed old, pale, and stiff. Three more televised debates followed. Many historians believe these debates swung the election in Kennedy's favor.

Only 43 years old, Kennedy was the youngest man ever to be elected president of the United States. He was also the country's first Roman Catholic president. To many Americans, Kennedy's election symbolized the beginning of a new era of optimism and vigor.

John F. Kennedy

Kennedy, the youngest man to be elected president, succeeded 70-year-old Dwight D. Eisenhower.

On January 20, 1961, Kennedy was **inaugurated** as the nation's 35th president. More than 20,000 people wrapped up against the bitter cold to attend the outdoor ceremony. Another 80 million watched the televised broadcast. With puffs of steam coming from his mouth, Kennedy delivered a speech that went down in history. He promised that the U.S. would "pay any price, bear any burden … in order to assure the survival and the success of liberty." In conclusion, he delivered a line that remains famous to this day: "And so, my fellow Americans: ask not what your country can do for you—ask what you can do for your country."

Kennedy entered office in the middle of the Cold War, a conflict between the democratic U.S. and the **communist** Soviet Union. This "war" did not involve direct fighting

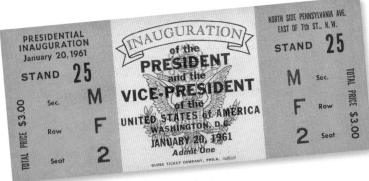

An original ticket to Kennedy's inauguration.

Starting as a barbed-wire fence in 1961, the Berlin Wall became a 12-foot (3.7 m) concrete obstacle.

between the two world superpowers. Instead, it was a struggle for worldwide influence. Both countries built up stockpiles of nuclear weapons. They also worked to spread their **ideologies** to other nations in Latin America, Asia, and Africa.

Communism had already taken hold in most of Eastern Europe. Kennedy was determined to keep it from spreading farther. He formed organizations such as the Peace Corps and the Alliance for Progress to provide aid to developing countries so that they would not turn to the Soviet Union. In Asia, Kennedy sent 16,000 troops to prevent Vietnam from falling into communist hands. He feared that if it did, it would cause a "domino effect," leading to the spread of communism across the continent.

The fight against communism took place closer to home as well. In 1961, Kennedy deployed 1,400 American-trained Cuban **exiles** to overthrow the communist leader of Cuba, **Fidel Castro**. In a disaster that became known as the Bay of Pigs, most of the rebels were captured or killed.

Only a year and a half later, in October 1962, U.S. spy planes discovered Soviet missile bases in Cuba. For 13 tense days, Americans expected a nuclear war against the Soviets to break out at any moment. But Kennedy skillfully negotiated with Soviet premier **Nikita Khrushchev**, and the missiles were removed. According to political analyst Larry Sabato, the resolution of the Cuban Missile Crisis "was probably [Kennedy's] finest moment as president."

Nikita Khrushchev

The struggle for Cold War supremacy extended even into space. In April 1961, the Soviet Union launched the first person into space. In response, Kennedy issued a new challenge to Americans: "I believe that this nation should commit itself to achieving the goal, before this decade is out, of landing a man on the moon and returning him safely to the Earth."

Even as he dealt with the worldwide tensions of the Cold War, Kennedy also faced a number of other issues. Racial unrest plagued the U.S. In the south, **segregation** was still widespread. During the first two years of his presidency, Kennedy stepped lightly around the **civil rights movement**. He didn't want to alienate Southerners in Congress. But in June 1963, Kennedy put together a civil rights bill. The legislation would ban discrimination

After John Glenn's historic orbiting in *Friendship 7 (pictured), Kennedy awarded him the Space Congressional Medal of Honor.*

in public places as well as in employment. It would also speed up the process of **integrating** schools. Despite Kennedy's push for the bill, by November it had stalled in Congress.

Kennedy's handling of the various crises of his presidency made him an extremely popular president. His approval ratings often climbed to near 80 percent. As much as Americans approved of Kennedy's work in office, though, they seemed even more captivated by the man himself. Kennedy's family added to his appeal. Women eagerly followed First Lady Jacqueline (best known as Jackie) Kennedy's elegant fashions. Newspapers printed pictures of the Kennedy

POINTING OUT

GROWING UP KENNEDY

*John F. Kennedy was born May 29, 1917, the second of nine children born to the wealthy family of Joseph and Rose Kennedy. Kennedy attended Harvard University, where he played football and suffered a back injury that would plague him the rest of his life. He worked for a time as an international reporter for his father, who was U.S. **ambassador** to the United Kingdom. During World War II, Kennedy served in the U.S. Navy. He was instrumental in saving the lives of his crew members after their patrol torpedo boat was destroyed by a Japanese warship. He entered politics soon after.*

Even as president, Kennedy vacationed with his wife and children at his family's summer home in Hyannis Port, Massachusetts.

children, Caroline and John Jr., playing in the Oval Office. Such pictures helped burnish Kennedy's image as a family man. (But after his death Americans learned that the president had had numerous affairs.) In August 1963, Jackie gave birth to the couple's third child, a son named Patrick. The premature baby's lungs were not fully developed, however, and he lived only two days.

Despite their grief, by November 1963, the president and first lady were ready to look ahead. The next election was only a year away, and it was time to start campaigning. Although she rarely accompanied her husband on political trips, Jackie agreed to appear in Texas with him. Some advisers warned Kennedy that it might be downright dangerous for him in Texas. Although it was Vice President Johnson's home state, many people there were hostile to the president—and especially his civil rights bill. But Kennedy insisted that no president should be afraid to travel anywhere in the U.S. And besides, he needed Texans' votes.

Hours before heading to Dallas, Kennedy gave a speech in a parking lot at the Hotel Texas in Fort Worth.

POINTING OUT

ASSASSINATED PRESIDENTS

John F. Kennedy was the fourth U.S. president to be assassinated in office. Abraham Lincoln was killed in 1865, James A. Garfield in 1881, and William McKinley in 1901. Several other presidents survived assassination attempts. A shooter aimed two pistols at Andrew Jackson, but both misfired. Theodore Roosevelt was shot in the chest while campaigning but was saved by a thick speech manuscript in his pocket. Assassins also tried and failed to get to Franklin Roosevelt and Harry Truman. Ronald Reagan was shot but survived, and gunmen fired at the White House during the presidencies of Bill Clinton, George W. Bush, and Barack Obama.

John and Jackie Kennedy, along with Johnson and his wife, Lady Bird, began their tour of Texas on November 21, 1963. They were escorted by Texas governor John Connally and his wife, Nellie. Crowds in San Antonio, Houston, and Fort Worth were enthusiastic and welcoming.

By late morning on November 22, there was only one city left to tour—Dallas. Jackie couldn't shake her worries about the city, where citizens proudly displayed "K.O. [Knock Out] the Kennedys" bumper stickers. Kennedy acknowledged that Dallas might be unfriendly, telling his wife, "We're heading into nut country today."

"But Jackie," he continued, "if somebody wants to shoot me from a window with a rifle, nobody can stop it, so why worry about it?" His words failed to reassure the First Lady.

CHAPTER TWO

EIGHT SECONDS IN DALLAS

At 11:40 A.M., Air Force One touched down at Dallas's Love Field. Cheers erupted from the crowd that had gathered as the First Lady, dressed in a pink suit and matching hat, stepped off the plane. The president followed close behind. The morning rain had cleared, and the sun warmed the day to a comfortable 63 °F (17.2 °C). Although no one in the crowd had been searched—not even the few who held signs calling the president a traitor—Kennedy and his wife walked over to shake hands.

Then they got into the back seat of the 21-foot-long (6.4 m), dark blue, presidential limousine. The car had been flown in from Washington, D.C., for the event. Governor Connally and his wife sat just in front of the first couple, on slightly lower "jump seats" that could be folded up when not in use. Although the limo could be fitted with a clear "bubble top," the beautiful weather meant that the top wouldn't be needed for the day's motorcade through downtown Dallas.

John Connally

15

Upon landing at Love Field, Elizabeth Cabell, wife of Dallas mayor Earle Cabell, presented Mrs. Kennedy with red roses.

The motorcade pulled away from Love Field at 11:55 A.M. to begin the 10-mile (16.1 km) route. **Secret Service** agents riding in cars immediately in front of and behind the president scanned the thick crowds that lined the streets. Their eyes roved over the 20,000 windows in the buildings along the way.

The motorcade route had been publicized in local newspapers, and an estimated 200,000 people had turned out to catch a glimpse of the president and his wife. Most cheered wildly as the limousine passed. The president ordered the car stopped twice—once to shake hands with a group of schoolchildren and once to greet a group of Catholic nuns.

By 12:30 P.M., the motorcade was nearing the end of its route. Nellie Connally turned to the president, saying, "You can't say that Dallas doesn't love you today, Mr. President." Kennedy smiled as the car turned onto Elm Street. The motorcade was now in front of Dealey Plaza, an open park surrounded by office buildings. Crowds here were thinner but still cheering enthusiastically.

Seconds after the car turned, a loud shot rang out, followed by another. The president reached up and grabbed his throat as a bullet tore through his neck. Governor Connally slumped in his seat. Just as Jackie reached for her husband, another shot blew up the side of the president's head. Blood, bone fragments, and brain matter splattered across the First Lady. Clint Hill, the

The Kennedys, enjoying the day's pleasant weather, greeted the crowds lining the streets of their motorcade route.

Secret Service agent assigned to protect Jackie, ran up behind the car and leapt across the trunk. He pushed the president and first lady down into the back seat as the limo tore off for nearby Parkland Hospital. The entire shooting had taken little more than eight seconds.

As the limo sped away, bystanders tried to make sense of what had just happened. Associated Press journalist Jack Bell, who was on the scene, described the chaos in an article printed in the *New York Times* that day: "There was a loud bang as though a giant firecracker had exploded in the caverns between the tall buildings we were just leaving behind us. In quick succession there were two other loud reports … like rifle shots." He looked around, trying to figure out where the shots had come from. Others were doing the same. Some thought the sounds had come from behind the president's limo. Others were sure the shots had been fired from up ahead. Hugh Aynesworth, a reporter for the *Dallas Morning News*, later remembered the moments immediately following the shots: "It was just complete chaos.… Nobody knew where the shots were coming from. Nobody knew who had been hit, if anybody. Nobody knew where to run to protect themselves."

Only minutes after the shots were fired, Merriman Smith, a United Press International (UPI) reporter, grabbed the press car's radio phone and sent out the first news of the shooting. The message went to news outlets around the country. At 12:40 P.M., CBS News anchor Walter Cronkite interrupted regular programming with a bulletin: "In Dallas, Texas, three shots were fired at President Kennedy's motorcade in downtown Dallas. The first reports say that President Kennedy has been seriously wounded by this shooting." Soon, radio and television stations across the nation were announcing the news. By

Clint Hill, the only Secret Service agent to reach the limo before it sped to the hospital, pushed the frantic Jackie down into the seat.

1:00 P.M., more than 75 million people knew about the shooting. Many stopped what they were doing to pray for the president's survival.

The doctors at Parkland Hospital knew that survival was unlikely, however. More than one-third of Kennedy's brain had been shot away. Although they worked feverishly to revive him, the case was hopeless. At 1:00 P.M., 30 minutes after the shooting, president John F. Kennedy was pronounced dead. (Governor Connally underwent several surgeries and eventually made a full recovery.)

At 1:33 P.M., White House assistant press secretary Malcolm Kilduff made the official announcement of the president's death. Five minutes later, the news traveled around the country as Cronkite, fighting back tears, reported, "From Dallas, Texas, the flash, apparently official, President Kennedy died at 1:00 P.M."

As the country was receiving word of the president's death, further drama was playing out in Dallas. Several eyewitnesses to the shooting had approached police officers. Some reported having seen a gun being pulled back into a sixth-floor window of the Texas School Book Depository, a book warehouse located on the corner of Elm and Houston streets. A couple people had even seen a man in the window. One bystander, Howard Brennan, was able to give

The following day, Kennedy's assassination was front-page news across the country.

police a description of the man: white, early 30s, about 5-foot-10 (1.8 m), and 160 to 170 pounds (72.6–77.1 kg). As the description went out over police radios, Dallas police officer Marrion Baker ran into the book depository. He met a man on the second floor and ordered him to stop. After being assured by the building manager that the man was Lee Harvey Oswald, an employee, the officer continued toward the roof.

Oswald exited the building undisturbed and made his way to Dallas's Oak Cliff neighborhood. There he was stopped by police officer J. D. Tippit at 1:18 P.M. Tippit got

POINTING OUT

THE FEW WHO CELEBRATED

Although people around the world mourned Kennedy's death, a few celebrated. In Alabama, a hotbed of racial tension, a young man called a radio station to say, "I feel sure … that Mr. Kennedy got exactly what he deserved. I'm sorry for his family. But I want to say that any man … who did what he did for [African Americans] should be shot." In Dallas and New York, also, some people expressed joy at the president's death. And in Cuba, Fidel Castro criticized Kennedy and his "hostile policies." He did, however, acknowledge that Cubans should "fight against systems, not the man."

Oswald served in the U.S. Marine Corps before moving to the Soviet Union in 1959, where he lived for nearly three years.

out of his car to question Oswald, whom the officer apparently thought matched the suspect's description. But Oswald pulled out a revolver and shot Tippit four times, killing him. Oswald fled the scene, but Johnny Calvin Brewer, a nearby shoe store manager, noticed him acting suspiciously. When Oswald ducked into the Texas Theater without paying, Brewer convinced the staff there to call the police.

Officers immediately swarmed the theater, and at 1:50 P.M., Oswald was arrested. The police knew they had caught Tippit's killer. Many suspected he was the president's assassin as well.

POINTING OUT

LEE HARVEY OSWALD

*Twenty-four-year-old Lee Harvey Oswald had been on the FBI's radar since 1959, when he **defected** to the Soviet Union. Agents questioned him after his return to the U.S. in 1962, but nothing he said raised a red flag. Even to his wife, Oswald showed no signs of disliking the president. Many historians have concluded that Oswald didn't decide to shoot Kennedy until only a few days before the assassination, when he learned that the president's motorcade would pass his workplace. Although no one will ever know why Oswald shot Kennedy, the Warren Commission speculated that he may have been trying "to find a place in history."*

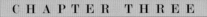

FOUR-DAY DRAMA

As word of the president's death spread, people everywhere were stunned. Drivers pulled over as they heard the news on their radios. People gathered around stores selling TVs to watch coverage through the windows. Offices and stores in some cities closed. Most people were devastated. Some wept in the streets. "It felt like your own heart had stopped and the whole world was standing still," said historian Martha Hodes. For many people, the president had seemed like someone they knew personally. "I feel like I've lost a real friend," a shoeshine man in Los Angeles told reporters. "I feel as if a member of my family had died, I really do," said a Detroit housewife.

The mourning wasn't restricted to the president's supporters. As Wilborn Hampton, a UPI reporter who was on the scene, said: "Whether you voted for him or not, he was a great symbol of a new America. He was bright and he was witty and he was handsome, and he carried so much hope for all of us who were young at that time. And he was gone just in a flash."

Nor was the shock and grief limited to America. "A flame went out for all those who had hoped for a just peace and a better life," said West Berlin mayor Willy Brandt when he learned of Kennedy's death. Even in the Soviet Union, schoolchildren left flowers at an impromptu memorial for the American president.

Gathered outside a radio shop in New York City, people waited for updates on the president's condition.

As of 2015, Lyndon B. Johnson was the only president to be sworn in both on a plane and by a woman.

Despite the country's grief, Lyndon Johnson—who automatically became president upon Kennedy's death—was determined to show the world that the American government would continue to function smoothly. At 2:40 P.M., Johnson took the presidential oath of office aboard Air Force One. With his wife on one side and Jackie Kennedy on the other, he repeated the words John F. Kennedy had said fewer than three years earlier, promising to "faithfully execute the office of President of the United States." Seven minutes later, Air Force One took off for Washington, D.C. Jackie Kennedy sat next to her husband's coffin. She refused to change out of her blood-spattered pink suit. "I want the world to see what Dallas has done to my husband," she said.

As soon as the plane landed, Kennedy's body was transported to Bethesda Naval Hospital for an **autopsy**. Afterward, the slain president's casket was placed in the East Room of the White House. Under Jackie's direction, White House entrances were draped in black, just as they had been after Abraham Lincoln's assassination 98 years earlier.

Meanwhile, in Dallas, police continued to collect evidence against Oswald. They found the gun used to assassinate the president hidden on the sixth floor of the Texas School Book Depository. At Oswald's house, they found a photo of him holding the gun, as well as an order form showing he had purchased the weapon by mail. In addition, Oswald's palm print was found on a cardboard box stacked near the window from which the shots had been fired.

By Saturday, November 23, Dallas police captain Will Fritz felt confident of the case against Oswald. "We're convinced beyond any doubt that he killed the president," Fritz told reporters. "I think the case is clinched." Dallas county district attorney Henry Wade thought the case would come to trial by January. He was determined to seek the death penalty.

Despite the mounting evidence against him, Oswald continued to deny the charges in police interrogations as well as during the many opportunities he was given to talk to the press. He insisted he was a patsy—someone meant to take the blame for another's crime.

On the morning of Sunday, November 24, nearly 70 police officers and 50 reporters jostled for space as Oswald was escorted into the basement garage of the Dallas police department. From there, he would be transferred to the county jail. Oswald had made it only about 10 feet (3 m) into the garage when a man stepped out of the crowd and shot him in the stomach at point-blank range. "He's been shot! He's been shot! Lee Oswald has been shot!" cried NBC correspondent Tom Pettit, broadcasting live from the scene.

Oswald was rushed to Parkland Hospital. Some of the same doctors who had tried to save Kennedy only two days earlier now worked on his

Thanks to the media frenzy surrounding
Oswald's arrest, thousands of Americans
saw Oswald get shot on live television.

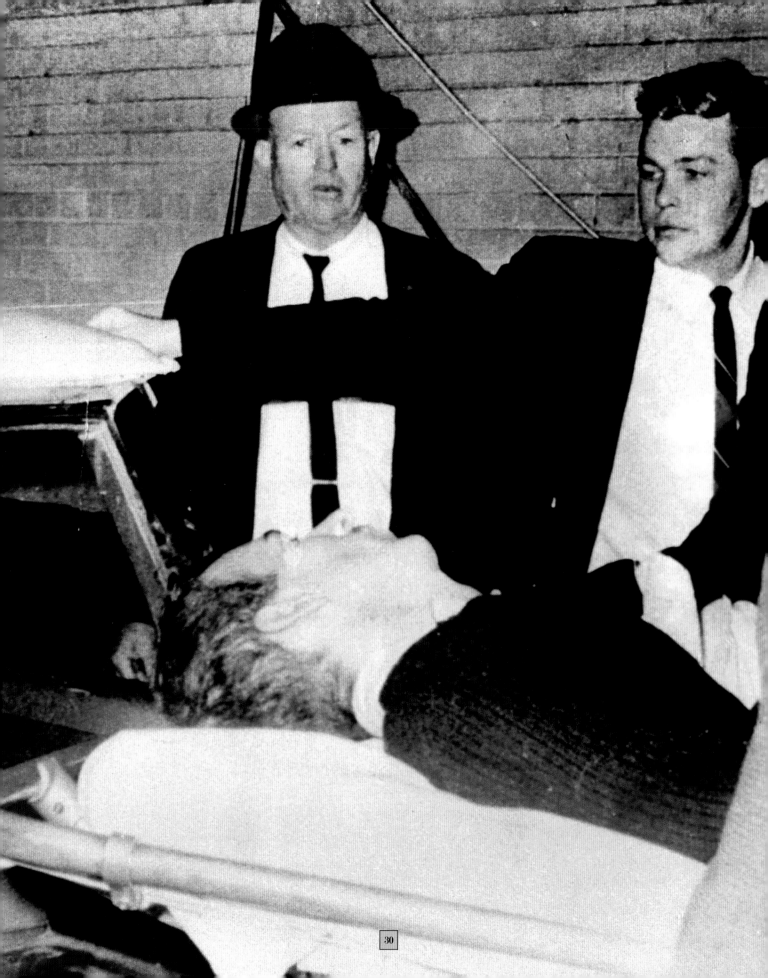

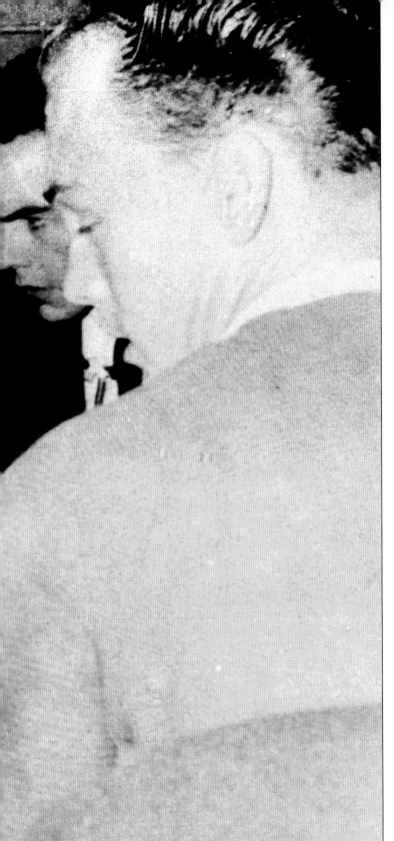

accused killer. They were unsuccessful. Oswald died at 1:07 P.M. His killer, Jack Ruby, a local nightclub owner, had been apprehended at the scene. He claimed to have shot Oswald in order to spare Jackie Kennedy the heartbreak of having to return to Dallas to testify at Oswald's murder trial.

But Ruby's murder of Oswald meant that the country would never know why Oswald had killed the president. And it made many people suspect that Oswald had been part of a larger conspiracy. They believed Ruby had been hired to keep Oswald from talking.

POINTING OUT

ANOTHER KENNEDY ASSASSINATION

*Among Kennedy's closest advisers during his time in the White House was his brother Robert, whom he had appointed attorney general. After Kennedy's assassination, Robert Kennedy was elected to the Senate. In 1968, he decided to try for the office that had cost his brother his life. On June 5, 1968, Robert Kennedy was in Los Angeles for the California **primary** election when he was shot in the head. He died the next day. His assassin, Sirhan B. Sirhan, was apprehended at the scene, but some Americans once again believed a conspiracy was involved in the death of a Kennedy.*

Oswald's shooter, Jack Ruby, later died of lung cancer while awaiting his second trial.

President Kennedy was buried in Arlington National Cemetery on his son's third birthday.

Among the conspiracy theories that circulated were that Oswald, a self-proclaimed communist, was in league with communists in the Soviet Union or Cuba. Others suggested that the conspirators were closer to home—the **mafia**, Federal Bureau of Investigation (FBI), Central Intelligence Agency (CIA), Dallas police, or even Vice President Johnson. Some said that Oswald wasn't the gunman at all but rather was set up. Others claimed that Oswald was one gunman but that he wasn't the only one who fired at the president.

The country had little time to focus on conspiracy theories on Sunday afternoon, though, as attention swung back to the assassinated president. An estimated 300,000 people lined D.C. streets to witness as Kennedy's casket was pulled by horse-drawn wagon to the U.S. Capitol. There it was placed on the **catafalque** that had held Lincoln's casket. Millions more watched the procession on television. After a Congressional memorial service, the Capitol was opened for public viewing of the casket. By that evening, the line to get into the building stretched to nine miles (14.5 km). Officials decided to keep

Following the flag-draped casket was a riderless horse, a symbol of a fallen leader or warrior who would ride no more.

the Capitol open through the night. By 9:00 A.M. on Monday, 250,000 people had filed past the president's casket.

That morning, the president's body was moved to St. Matthew's Cathedral. Jackie Kennedy walked with her husband's brothers, attorney general Robert Kennedy and senator Edward Kennedy, behind the casket. They were followed by a procession of 220 foreign officials from 92 countries. One million people lined the streets to watch the procession. Nearly the entire rest of the country watched it on television. After the funeral at St. Matthew's, Kennedy was buried at Arlington National Cemetery. Although the assassination story seemed to be over, Kennedy's legacy was just beginning.

POINTING OUT

MOVING ON

After Kennedy's death, Jackie and the children moved to the Washington, D.C., neighborhood of Georgetown. But their home was constantly mobbed by tourists and the media. In the summer of 1964, they relocated to New York City. In October 1968, Jackie married Aristotle Onassis, a Greek millionaire. Soon afterward, she took up a career as a book editor. She died of cancer in 1994. The Kennedys' daughter Caroline grew up to become a lawyer, author, and editor. John Jr. also became a lawyer and started the political magazine George. He died in a plane crash in 1999.

A LASTING LEGACY

On November 27, 1963—only two days after Kennedy's funeral—President Johnson spoke before a joint session of Congress. He urged legislators to keep America moving forward, just as Kennedy had wanted. "This is our challenge—not to hesitate, not to pause, not to turn about and linger over this evil moment, but to continue on our course so that we may fulfill the destiny that history has set for us. Our most immediate tasks are here on this Hill," he said. He urged Congress to "honor President Kennedy's memory" by bringing about "the earliest possible passage of the civil rights bill for which he fought so long." By doing so, Johnson said, they could ensure "that John Fitzgerald Kennedy did not live—or die—in vain."

Johnson's speech had the desired effect. Congress soon passed the **Civil Rights Act of 1964**—a much stronger version of the bill it had failed to act on while Kennedy was alive. The next year, Johnson secured passage of the **Voting Rights Act of 1965**.

Although Johnson was praised for continuing and expanding Kennedy's work on civil rights, he

Lyndon B. Johnson

In his first speech to Congress as president, Johnson was frequently interrupted by applause and received an ovation.

Johnson's good favor did not last, especially as the conflict escalated in Vietnam and anti-war demonstrations grew.

was also widely criticized for escalating American involvement in Vietnam. By 1968, Johnson had increased Kennedy's 16,000 troops in that country to 535,000. The new president insisted that he was only following Kennedy's policy for the region. However, critics contended that Kennedy had been looking for ways to withdraw from further involvement in Vietnam.

Even as Johnson spurred Congress to enact Kennedy's legislation, he also launched a large-scale investigation into the president's murder. On November 29, 1963, Johnson created a commission to investigate and report on all

POINTING OUT

SIXTH-FLOOR MUSEUM

Immediately following the president's assassination, Dallas leaders called for the Texas School Book Depository to be torn down. But the building remained standing, and its lower floors are today used as county offices. In 1989, the sixth floor was turned into a museum—called simply The Sixth Floor Museum at Dealey Plaza. The museum holds more than 45,000 items related to Kennedy's assassination, including original photographs and film footage. From the museum's windows, visitors can look out on Elm Street, where a large painted X marks the spot where Kennedy was shot in the head. Only a few blocks away is the Conspiracy Museum.

aspects of the assassination. Headed by Supreme Court chief justice Earl Warren, the group came to be known as the Warren Commission. For the next 10 months, the Warren Commission reviewed evidence gathered by the FBI, Secret Service, Dallas Police Department, and other organizations. It interviewed eyewitnesses and looked into Oswald's past. Among the key pieces of evidence studied was a 26-second film of the event taken by a bystander named Abraham Zapruder. The film captured the instant the final bullet shattered the president's skull.

Based on the evidence, the Warren Commission concluded that three shots had been fired from the sixth floor of the Texas School Book Depository. The first shot was found to have missed the presidential limo entirely. The Commission speculated that the second bullet passed through Kennedy's back before exiting through his throat and then striking Governor Connally. It hit the governor in the back, came out through his chest, reentered his wrist, and finally lodged in his thigh. The third bullet hit the president's skull. This theory, which became known as the "single bullet" or "magic bullet" theory, for its insistence that a single bullet hit both Kennedy and Connally, was widely questioned. Even three members of the Warren Commission were skeptical of it, as (secretly) was President Johnson.

Gathered at Dealey Plaza, onlookers observed a re-creation of Kennedy's assassination that provided evidence to the Warren Commission.

The Warren Commission's most important finding was that Oswald was, indeed, Kennedy's killer and that he had acted alone. "The Commission has found no evidence that Lee Harvey Oswald or Jack Ruby was part of any conspiracy, domestic or foreign, to assassinate President Kennedy," the Commission's report said. The 300,000-word report, issued in September 1964, put many minds to rest—but not everyone's.

Many people pointed out flaws in the initial investigation as well as in the Warren Commission's methods. For example, the crime

POINTING OUT

INTERPRETING THE EVIDENCE

In 1976, Congress tasked the House Select Committee on Assassinations (HSCA) with reinvestigating Kennedy's murder. Much of the HSCA's investigation confirmed the findings of the Warren Commission. But an acoustics expert consulted by the committee claimed to detect at least five gunshots on an audio recording of the assassination. Based on this, the HSCA concluded that Kennedy was "probably assassinated as a result of a conspiracy." The committee theorized that there had been a second shooter. The HSCA's conclusion was discredited upon further analysis, which determined that the sounds identified as gunshots on the recording occurred after the assassination.

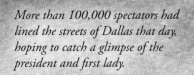

More than 100,000 spectators had lined the streets of Dallas that day, hoping to catch a glimpse of the president and first lady.

scene was not closed immediately after the shooting, so evidence could have been tampered with. In addition, after bringing the president into the hospital, Secret Service agents washed down the back seat of the limousine—wiping away blood and other important **forensic** evidence in the process. The autopsy carried out at Bethesda Naval Hospital was criticized as being rushed and inadequate. It was performed by doctors who had never before autopsied a gunshot victim. The Warren Commission was faulted for failing to interview a number of eyewitnesses, some of whom claimed they heard shots from a bridge in front of the president or a grassy knoll to the side of the motorcade. Political analyst Larry Sabato points out, though, that such problems with the investigation "do not automatically mean that the Commission erred in fingering Oswald as the lone gunman. Much testimony supports the Commission viewpoint."

Even so, many people held firm to the belief that a conspiracy surrounded Kennedy's death. Part of the reason for this, says historian Thomas Reed Turner, is that "it is more satisfying to believe that Kennedy died as a victim of a cause rather than at the hands of a deranged gunman."

Suspicion of the government was a relatively new phenomenon in 1963 America, but it has continued to the present day. In fact, many mark the Kennedy assassination as the end of

An eternal flame, lit by Jackie during the funeral, still burns at the head of Kennedy's grave in Arlington.

JOHN FITZGERALD KENNEDY

1917 — 1963

an era of optimism and the beginning of American cynicism and distrust in the federal government.

In addition to changing American attitudes toward the government, the assassination marked the rise of television news. All three major networks—CBS, NBC, and ABC—provided continuous coverage of the assassination and related events for four days, without commercial interruption. The cost in lost revenue is estimated to have been $40 million. According to *Entertainment Weekly*, Kennedy's assassination made America into "a TV nation." An estimated 175 million people (out of a total population of 189 million) huddled around television sets, waiting to learn the newest developments and to share their grief.

Today, more than 50 years after the assassination, Kennedy is well remembered. Streets and schools around the world bear his name. More than 1,300 memorials to the slain president have been erected in the U.S. and worldwide. Nearly 1,000 books have been written about his assassination.

Few historians consider Kennedy among the great presidents. He was in office too short a time to have made any major achievements. Many do note, however, his role in spurring Americans to land a man on the moon (a goal that was achieved six years after his death, in 1969). And the Peace Corps remains as a legacy of Kennedy's challenge to the American people to "ask not" but to "do for your country."

Despite historians' opinions, the majority of Americans rank Kennedy as the greatest U.S. president, alongside Abraham Lincoln. Many wonder how world events might have differed if Kennedy had lived to serve out his term. There is no way to know. And that, perhaps more than anything, is why many people consider this a turning point in history.

May 29, 1917	John Fitzgerald Kennedy is born in Brookline, Massachusetts, the second of Joseph and Rose Kennedy's nine children.
August 1943	Kennedy saves his crew after their navy patrol boat is destroyed by a Japanese warship.
November 5, 1946	Kennedy is elected to the House of Representatives.
November 4, 1952	Kennedy is elected to the U.S. Senate.
September 12, 1953	Kennedy marries Jacqueline "Jackie" Bouvier.
November 8, 1960	In a close election, Kennedy becomes the youngest man and first Catholic ever elected president.
January 20, 1961	At his inauguration as 35th president, Kennedy tells Americans to "ask what you can do for your country."
April 17, 1961	Kennedy sends 1,400 Cuban exiles to invade Cuba at the Bay of Pigs, but the invasion fails.
September 12, 1962	Kennedy challenges Americans to land a man on the moon before the end of the decade.
October 1962	During the Cuban Missile Crisis, Kennedy tries to prevent nuclear war after Soviet missile bases are discovered in Cuba.
November 22, 1963	Kennedy is assassinated in Dallas, and Lyndon B. Johnson is sworn in as president.
November 24, 1963	Lee Harvey Oswald, Kennedy's assassin, is killed by Jack Ruby.
November 25, 1963	After a funeral at St. Matthew's Cathedral, Kennedy is buried at Arlington National Cemetery.
November 27, 1963	President Johnson urges Congress to take action on the civil rights bill and other legislation as a tribute to Kennedy.
September 24, 1964	The Warren Commission issues its report on Kennedy's assassination.

ambassador—an official who represents his or her government in another nation

autopsy—a medical examination of a dead body to determine the cause of death

catafalque—a wooden framework, often draped with cloth, used to support a coffin for public viewing

Civil Rights Act of 1964—bill passed by Congress in 1964 outlawing discrimination based on race, religion, or national origin

civil rights movement—political movement of the 1950s and 1960s with the goal of attaining equal treatment for racial minorities

communist—involving a system of government in which all property and business is owned and controlled by the state, with the goal of creating a classless society

conspiracy—a secret plan carried out by two or more people

defected—left one's own country, often because of disagreement with its policies, to live in an opposing or enemy country

exiles—people who live away from their home country, either by choice or as a form of punishment

Fidel Castro—political leader of Cuba who came to power in 1959 by overthrowing the government of dictator Fulgencio Batista and remained in power until 2008; under Castro, Cuba became the first communist nation in the Western Hemisphere

forensic—having to do with the use of science to investigate and prosecute crimes

ideologies—the sets of beliefs that form the basis of specific political, social, or economic systems

inaugurated—formally installed in an office through a ceremony

integrating—ending segregation by intermixing majority and minority populations; school integration involved allowing African American students to attend schools with white students

mafia—a secret organization involved in drug dealing, gambling, and other illegal activities

Nikita Khrushchev—leader of the Soviet Union from 1953–64, who sought a policy of "peaceful coexistence" with the U.S.

primary—a special election in which voters choose among candidates from the same political party to run in a general election against candidates from other political parties

Secret Service—department of the U.S. government responsible for protecting the president and his family

segregation—the process of separating people by race; in the U.S., segregation meant that African Americans had to ride at the back of buses, eat in separate dining establishments, and attend separate schools

Voting Rights Act of 1965—legislation enacted to prohibit racial discrimination in voting; the act outlawed the use of literacy tests to determine voter eligibility

Bugliosi, Vincent. *Reclaiming History: The Assassination of President John F. Kennedy*. New York: W. W. Norton, 2007.

Life. *The Day Kennedy Died: 50 Years Later LIFE Remembers the Man and the Moment*. New York: Time Home Entertainment, 2013.

Newseum. *President Kennedy Has Been Shot: Experience the Moment-to-Moment Account of Four Days that Changed America*. Naperville, Ill.: Soucebooks Mediafusion, 2003.

O'Reilly, Bill, and Martin Dugard. *Killing Kennedy: The End of Camelot*. New York: Henry Holt, 2012.

Sabato, Larry J. *The Kennedy Half-Century: The Presidency, Assassination, and Lasting Legacy of John F. Kennedy*. New York: Bloomsbury, 2013.

Semple, Robert B. Jr., ed. *Four Days in November: The Original Coverage of the John F. Kennedy Assassination by the Staff of* The New York Times. New York: St. Martin's, 2003.

Swanson, James. *End of Days: The Assassination of John F. Kennedy*. New York: William Morrow, 2013.

The Warren Commission Report: The Official Report of the President's Commission on the Assassination of President John F. Kennedy. 1964. Stamford, Conn.: Longmeadow Press, 1992.

The History Place: John F. Kennedy Photo History

http://www.historyplace.com/kennedy/

This history of Kennedy's life includes photographs of his childhood and war years, as well as his political career and presidency.

The Sixth Floor Museum at Dealey Plaza

http://www.jfk.org

The online collection of the Sixth Floor Museum includes photographs and film footage from Kennedy's life and assassination.

Note: Every effort has been made to ensure that the websites listed above are suitable for children, that they have educational value, and that they contain no inappropriate material. However, because of the nature of the Internet, it is impossible to guarantee that these sites will remain active indefinitely or that their contents will not be altered.